WROCŁAW
THE MEETING PLACE

PHOTOGRAPHS
STANISŁAW KLIMEK

TEXT
BEATA MACIEJEWSKA

WYDAWNICTWO VIA NOVA

The Oder, by which thou layest and by the restless current of which
thou breakest into many streams,
that from their source to their estuary
or flowing through all northern lands –
findeth nowhere one to rival thee
O Wrocław[1]

thus wrote Barthel (Bartholomäus) Stein, author of a 16th Century description of the city of Wrocław. And since he was a man who travelled a lot – he studied in Cracow and Wien, worked in Wittenberg and Leipzig – his words are surely worthy of belief...

He was not the first person to be ravished by the city on the Oder. In a book written for the Sicilian King Roger the Arab geographer al-Edrisi praised Wrocław as "a city famous for its scholars and craftsmen", and a Franciscan pilgrim Antonius even went as far as saying that "Jerusalem is as big as Wrocław but not built as beautifully".

From the beginning of its existence Wrocław was a target of desire, hence it is no wonder that it has changed hands so many times. The city has belonged by turns to Czechs, Poles, Hungarians, Austrians and Germans. Walloons, Jews, Italians, Ruthenians settled here and the different nations, religions and cultures mixed and mingled to such a degree that today it is often impossible to judge unequivocally what is whose work. It is a place in which one can see the history of Europe as in a microscopic lens. Silesia – called "a land of bridges" and "land of encounters" – and its capital have always been located "between" and there in lies one of Wrocław's chief virtues thanks to which the city has become a portal through which East meets with West.

Ostrów Tumski (the Cathedral Island) is Wrocław's place of birth. It was here that 10th Century planners, most probably Czechs seeking to fortify the frontier of their territory, chose to erect the first buildings. Archaeologists base this claim on the words of German folklorist Fritz Enderwitz stated that it was the Polish ruler, Mieszko, who founded the city. This worshipper of pagan gods was born blind and desired only two things – to recover his sight and perpetuate his family's line. In order to achieve at least one of these ambitions he decided to marry the Czech Princess Dobrawa. He travelled to the territory of the present day Wrocław to meet his bride and when a cortege of his Christian fiancee arrived in the forest clearing Mieszko swore fealty to the new God where upon his eyesight returned and he beheld for the first time the beautiful visage of Dobrawa and promptly fell in love. On the site where he recovered his sight, Mieszko founded Piast Wrocław.

Wrocław together with the whole of Silesia was incorporated into the Piast state before 990, in the latter part of the Mieszko I's life, following the death of Dobrawa when the Polish ruler was no longer bound by fealty to his Czech father-in-law, prince Bolesław I Přemyslid.

The first reference to Wrocław dates from the year 1000 from the hand of bishop Thietmar of Merseburg. The bishop, while describing the pilgrimage of Emperor Otto III to the tomb of St. Vojtech mentioned the creation of an ecclesiastical organisation on the territory of the state of Bolesław Chrobry (the Brave), Mieszko I's son. He described Wrocław as a seat of one of the three bishoprics subordinate to the metropolis in Gniezno. On one occasion he referred to the city as Wrotizla and on the other as Wortizlava. This appellation is derived from the name Wrocisław or "he who is to return famous". Unfortunately, there is little in the history and legends to suggest who Wrocisław was. Poles maintain that he may have been a local tribal leader, while Czechs believe him to have been the prince Vratislav who ruled between 915 and 921.

However, one thing is certain: that Wrocław has gained the renown promised by its name and its choice as the capital of the bishopric and its importance to the Piast monarchy. The chronicler Gall Anonim (the

Wrocław's coat of arms was granted to the city in 1530 by the Czech and Hungarian King Ferdinand I, and was later approved by Emperor Charles V. In the centre is the head of St. John the Baptist, patron saint of the city and the cathedral. In the top left-hand corner a rearing lion in a crown, the symbol of the Czech king, next to which is the Silesian eagle. Below is a bust of St. John the Evangelist on the upturned crown. The 'W' letter in Wrocław's coat of arms alludes to a legendary founder of the city named Wratislav (Wratysław). (The coat of arms of 1616, the western façade of the City Hall, contemporary photograph.)

Illustration on page 1:
Wrocław's Main Square is one of the biggest in Europe and was delineated after the Mongol invasion of 1241. In the foreground, in the centre of the Square, is the New City Hall erected at the end of the 19th century, now the seat of Wrocław's Mayor and local authorities. In the photograph is the Main Square during the final concert of an annual national charity action called the Great Orchestra of Christmas Aid (12 January 2003).

[1] The name of the city changed many times in its history, the Latin name was Wratislavia, the German name used till 1945 was Breslau. A contemporary name is used in the text.

Images of St. John the Baptist can be seen on houses throughout Wrocław as well as on paving stones and public utility buildings. He is the patron saint of the cathedral and the city. The oldest representation of the saint dates back to around 1160. In the 15th century it was placed on the northern wall of the cathedral. Nowadays we may see a replica there. The original, damaged during the bombardment of the city by Russian aircraft at Easter 1945, is kept in the Archdiocesan Museum (contemporary photograph).

The foundation tympanum in the Church of Our Lady on the Sand (around 1150) shows Maria Włostowicowa (Mary Wlast) and her son Świętosław, dedicating the church to the Holy Virgin. The figures of the founders are almost the same height as the figure of St. Mary (contemporary photograph).

Anonymous) mentions the city as the main seats of the Kingdom of Poland – "sedes regni principales". Already in the first half of the 11th Century the capital of the whole Silesia, because a deputy of the monarch was at the office in Wrocław, *comes provinciae*.

The Main Square constitutes the heart of the city, which was founded at the intersection of important European transportation routes from the South – from the Czech side – to the North and from the western Europe towards the East. International trade was blossoming here from the very beginnings of the history, inhabitants of Wrocław were getting richer thanks to this, and so was the city, to the safe of which huge sums from the taxes were pouring. In the 15th Century Wrocław more people traded here than in Prague, Ypres, Brno or Frankfurt am Main. One could always meet guests from around the world – Italians, Lithuanians, Ruthenians, as well as Poles from Mazovia, Wielkopolska and Małopolska. The Building of Great Weight (a commemorative plaque is laid on its foundations today) was always surrounded by dusty carts, bales of wool, barrels with alum, tallow and salt.

Although situated far from the coast, in their search for new markets the merchants of Wroclaw took to the sea. It is known that the City Council of Wrocław asked the authorities of Stralsund for help because a ship bearing broadcloth owned by two citizens of the Lower Silesian capital has crashed in the vicinity of Szczecin and was threatened with confiscation of its goods on the grounds of *ius naufragii* (the right to ownership of items cast onto land by the sea).

The inhabitants of Wrocław traded with Scandinavian countries, in this way delivering herrings to the Silesian tables, as well as venturing into the vicinity of Scotland. The names of medieval tenement-houses at New Market – Helsingör, Skanör and Rosehaupt – attest this contact with Scandinavian countries. In 1387 Wrocław became a member of The Hanse League, the largest association of North German, Rhenish, Teutonic, Swedish and Polish cities which monopolised contemporary North European trade and became a real political power. The Piast rulers took effective care of the development of Wrocław as a European craft and trade center.

The importance of the city increased under the reign of the Piast Duke Henryk IV the Righteous (Probus). Although he died suddenly at the age of 33 (he was probably poisoned) he did manage to bestow the city with many privileges – in 1271 he allowed the construction of sixteen bread stalls, two years later he agreed to set up thirty two further stalls and he also granted the city with the monopoly for transporting barrels of beer and profits resulting from this privilege. Wrocław also received from Probus the right to set up a lead melting plant and utilisation of the lead weight which was previously located in the city of Frankenstein. Along with a device for weighing lead the Silesian metropolis was granted the 'Warehousing Right' which meant that all goods in transit had to be offered for sale in Wrocław. Thus, precious eastern and Italian silk fabrics, thin Flanders-broadcloth, weapons and decorative articles, herrings from the Baltic Sea, copper and iron from Hungary and salt from the mines of Little Poland in Bochnia and Wieliczka. Only goods remaining unpurchased after three days were allowed to be transported further by foreign merchants.

Duke Henryk IV (the Righteous) also left one of the most splendid sanctuaries in Silesia – the Saint Cross Collegiate. However, prior to its foundation a quarrel between the Duke and the Bishop of Wrocław, Thomas II, led to the expulsion of the latter, the demolition of his castle in the town of Neisse and cereal from ecclesiastical granaries being used as horse feed. When Thomas subsequently fell to his knees and begged forgiveness the Duke suddenly repented and in the closing act of the argument ordered the Saint Cross Church to be raised on Ostrów Tumski.

The Duke's quarrel with Bishop Thomas was primarily over ownership of villages located by ecclesiastical hierarchs on ducal lands and a difference in attitude towards the institution of marriage: the Duke, then in his twenties, had fallen in love with Matilda, the charming daughter of a Brandenburg margrave and had sent his current wife, a duchess of Oppeln, back to her relatives, causing grave insult. Moreover, he proceeded to marry Matilda, breaking all ecclesiastical rules and meeting the resistance of the bishop. However, he was inconsistent in his feelings and while he continued to love Matilda to the end of his days ("her body is a of great ruptures", as he claimed in a poem written in German) he returned the disputed property and made the bishop the executor of his last will.

Henryk IV the Righteous had to wait a long time for appreciation. Eventually nineteenth-century, Polish historians made him the hero of a black legend. "A germanised descendent of Bolesław Chrobry the Brave"

– taunted the Duke Karol Szajnocha, chronicler of Polish history as he reproached the ruler for composing and singing German love songs. Poles also accused Henryk of favouring German settlers and townspeople and criticised the struggle with the bishop of Wrocław in which "everything which was German, sided with the Duke". Even more interestingly, the poet Tanshauser, a contemporary of Henryk claimed that "Uz Polen lande ein Fuerste war, den will ich loben sicherlich" ("From Polish land was this Duke whom I wish to praise), and Nazis exhumed the Dukes remains and subjected them to analysis at an anthropological institute to determine if he had been sufficiently "Germanic".

This strange history of the Duke reflected the spirit of the city of Wrocław which was slowly being settled by various national groups including Poles, German settlers brought by Duke Henryk I the Bearded under the *melioratio terrae*, Walloon weavers, Jews and Czechs. Their respective cultures permeated the city and it is often difficult to ascribe particular architectural and artistic works to any single one of them. In the collection of Wrocław University Library, for example, there is a 15th Century *Codex* of Nicholas from the town of Cosel in which an indecent Polish-Czech song about a maid who did not want to give oats to a horse. Many Czech scholars attribute these obscenities to the work of Poles while some Poles maintain that the song is in fact of Czech origin.

The frontier city has always attracted the restless souls of various nations – adventurous people dreaming about a big success as well as eminent intellectuals. Peter Wlast, a Polish magnate and outstanding mind of medieval Wrocław was said to have come from Denmark, taken part in Viking expeditions and married the daughter of the French King. He achieved the pinnacle of success in his lifetime and then lost everything. The administrator of the Province of Silesia, Magnus, was to be acknowledged as the legal son of the English King Harold II (who was slain after the Battle of Hastings which commenced the Norman invasion of England under the leadership of William I the Conqueror, Duke of Normandy in 1066), while the bishop Walter who instigated the construction of Wrocław Cathedral came from Malonne at Sambre.

The ethnic diversity of Wrocław, and more precisely the escalating expansion of Germans was bound to generate tensions. In 1327 the use of Polish language in disputes over debts was forbidden. The new customs tariff was written in German and the Polish language was systematically eliminated from courts, though strong economic links with Poland meant that the citizens of Wrocław were often bilingual.

Henry IV the Righteous, the Duke of Wrocław and Kraków ordered that he be buried in the collegiate church of the Holy Cross. His sarcophagus was transferred to the National Museum after the war. It is now empty because the duke's remains were taken by Nazis so that the Institute of Anthropology could examine Germanity of the Piast duke. However, before this matter could be resolved, the building with its contents was destroyed during a Soviet bombardment (archival photograph from around 1930).

THE CITY OF GREAT CAREERS

The incorporation of Wrocław into the Kingdom of Bohemia in 1335 did not significantly change the ethnic composition of the city. The change of national status could be told mainly by the nationality of domestic clerks – starting from a Starost of Wrocław (subsequently Silesian) to junior administrative clerks. Although the municipal book mentions townsmen by the surname of Prager or Czechynne, Czechs did not feel particularly attracted to the city of Wrocław. They preferred to remain in Prague and to trade with the Silesian metropolis. On the other hand, patricians, whose ancestors came to Wrocław from German cities, mainly Nuremberg occupied important positions while the Polish element predominated among commoners, minor merchants and craftsmen.

Even so, Wrocław remained a city where great careers could be enjoyed by people from the outside. One such person was Heinrich von Rybisch who was born and brought up in a poor family, which wandered to the city of Wrocisław from as far away as Büdingen in Saxony. Outstandingly intelligent and well educated at German Universities he was also endowed by Divinity with a pragmatic cleverness. In 1520 – at the age of 36 – he became a syndic of Wrocław and soon after a general tax-collector for the Duchy of Wrocław and Oppeln. The position of general tax-collector for the whole Silesia and Lusatian Margrave as well as imperial advisor crowned his career. His house followed contemporary Italian fashions and was the first of such design to be constructed in Silesia and perhaps north of the Alps. It was situated on present-day Ofiar Oświęcimskich street (then called Junkernstrasse) at numbers 1–3. However, the overt display of haughtiness which the house represented found little liking among the citizens of the city. Rybisch attempted to settle this dispute with his compatriots by mounting the following inscription on the portal of his house: "Be pious, without envy or hatred, and so being build yourself a better one and leave this one for me". Rumours circulated that stones from demolition of the St. Vincent Abbey on Elbing, which was the foundation of Peter Wlast, had been used

Only the portal of the historic house of Heinrich Rybisch, one of the most influential men in the 16th century Wrocław, has survived to the present. In its day this Renaissance house more closely resembled a palace than a burgher's house and aroused the envy of the townspeople (contemporary photograph).

The low relief built into the wall of St. Elisabeth's Church commemorates falling down of a tower on 24 February 1529. Witnesses claimed that the tower was caught by angels and put on Wrocław's cobblestones, thanks to which nobody was hurt (contemporary photograph).

in its construction. And indeed Rybisch, a patron and collector, boasting a surname of Philocalos (beauty lover), did contribute, under the pretence of Turkish threat, to the demolition of the Roman cloister. The tomb of the founder and his wife Mary was destroyed by this way, and their skulls were used for bowling.

Heinrich von Rybisch was, after all, a Protestant as was the entire City Council, and he lived during that turbulent period of religious discord known as The Reformation. Thus every wile and deception was countenanced in order to suppress the Catholic Church, even the exaggerated claim that invading Turks could use the cloister as a stronghold. Occasionally religious antagonism took amusing turns. When in 1520 a hurricane knocked down a spire of the Elizabeth Church which had been handed-over to the Protestants four years previously, Catholics trumpeted that God had vented his wrath at the relinquishing of His sacred temple into the hands of heretics. Protestants, on the other hand, claimed that it was a sign of Divine guardianship because the only casualty of the catastrophe had been a cat. It was not long before eye-witnesses emerged stating that they had seen angels seize the falling tower and direct the debris over the Market Square.

Even so, one is forced to admit that The Reformation in the capital of the Lower Silesia steered a fairly mild course which significantly contributed to the emergence of an atmosphere of religious tolerance and dialogue between different faiths, a characteristic so typical of modern Wrocław. Contemporary Wrocław continues this tradition as is evidenced by the creation of the Mutual Respect District a few years ago. A Synagogue, an Orthodox church, a Protestant chapel as well as a Catholic Church are situated wall to wall, and followers of each denomination visit one another and organise joint charity campaigns.

Under Bohemian rule Wrocław not only underwent further economic development but also flourished culturally. It was at this time that the idea of founding a university was first conceived, finding its earliest advocates in legatus a latere cardinal Piotr Isvalies, Wrocław councillor Hans Haunold and in a municipal scribe named Mohrenberg. The well-known printer and bookbinder Conrad Baumgarten from Rothenburg took this vision so much to heart that he gave up Leipzig for Wrocław. All signs seemed favourable. On 20th July 1505 the King of Bohemia and Hungary issued a university foundation privilege in Buda. The four-faculty university was to be laic, and the City Council would extend patronage over it. Unfortunately, Pope Julius II forbade the foundation of a university in Wrocław even though the inhabitants of the city had sent three thousand florins to Rome to receive the confirmation and papal edict. However, the Polish King Alexander Jagiellon lodged a formal protest and support for the university which would have vied with the University of Cracow was eliminated.

The project was given a new lease of life two centuries later while Wrocław was under the rule of the Austrian Habsburgs (since 1526). This time the Jesuits took the initiative and it proved successful. However, it was not an easy thing to achieve. The City Council of Wrocław, which was made up of Protestants, sent a petition to the Emperor Leopold requesting that the opening of the University be banned. Councillors voiced warnings of riots and about the licentiousness of students who were impossible to restrain. The City Council was primarily afraid of recatholisation, but it was also true that the city ha had problems with under-invested pupils or students. The City Council sent representatives to Vienna in November 1965 and tried to obstruct the Jesuits' efforts by offering tempting gifts. However, the inauguration of the University was a foregone thing but also one which, due to financial difficulties, was delayed until after 15th November 1702.

The intellectual culture of the sixteenth and seventeenth century Wrocław was very sophisticated indeed, and Wrocław was worthy of a university for this reason. The Wrocław humanists congregated around Craton von Krafftheim (the adjutant doctor of three Austrian emperors – Ferdinand I, Maximilian II and Rudolf II) carried a great deal of clout with the Habsburgs. Also such poets as Jacob Monavius and Andreas Calagius, botanist Carolus Clusius (official collector of plants for emperor Maximilian II) and Andreas Dudith, a Hungarian diplomat who maintained lively contact with French humanists belonged to this circle.

Martin Opitz (in 1624 he published *Buch von der deutschen Poeterei*, a fundamental theoretical text on German Renaissance poetry), Andreas Gryphius or Johannes Scheffler, known under the pseudonym of Angelius Silesius – the Silesian Angel all went down in history of literature. The latter was derived from Wrocław stock in the first generation because his father Stanislaus was a Cracow townsman. At this point it is pertinent to quote the praise of Philipp Melanchton (a co-founder of the Lutheranism doctrine), who considered the *erudition and education of the inhabitants* and the *carefulness and integrity in managing the city affairs and solicitude along with humanitarianism of social standard* [„Die grösste Zierde der Stadt sind die Gelehrsamkeit und die Bildung ihrer Bürger, die Sorgsamkeit und die Gerechtigkeit im Regiment der Stadt, die Sorgfalt und Humanität in der Regelung der Sitten"] to be the greatest virtues of Wrocław.

Also worthy of attention is the fact that in 1666 a Municipal polish school was opened for the children of Wrocław's mercantile families. Earlier still, in 1616, a *Key to Polish and German Language* [*Schlüssel zur Polnischen und Teutschen Sprache*] was compiled by Jeremiah Rotter . The author explained that "a textbook for teaching Polish language here and throughout Silesia, and particularly to all merchants, hospitable hosts and craftsmen" is urgently needed for trading purposes (until the time of the First World War it was custom for shops to employ at least one Polish-speaking assistant for the comfort and convenience of Polish clientele). Indeed, commerce remained the source of Wrocław's prosperity until 1741 when the Prussian King Frederick Hohenzollern annexed Wrocław along with the rest of Silesia.

A COSMOPOLITAN METROPOLIS

The city did not intend to defend itself and promptly regretted supporting Frederick who, like a conqueror pillaging a vanquished foe, proceeded to empty the purses of the city's inhabitants. Transit trade, which up until then had represented a valuable source of revenue for Wrocław now began to deteriorate rapidly as Silesian goods as well as those being transported through the region became the objects on which burdensome excise taxes were levied. Despite this decrease in profits it was the annulment of their political freedoms and privileges which was most painful for the inhabitants of Wrocław to bear.

The Statue for the city of Wrocław [*Ratshäusliches Reglement für die Stadt Breslau*], which the Prussian king issued on 27th January 1748 abolished the former city council which had been appointed on a yearly basis, and introduced a permanent governing assembly in its place, the so called municipality. The municipal authorities, the members of which were nominated constituted a branch of the state apparatus and were thus less concerned with the care and prosperity of Wroclaw than they were with the Prussian state treasury and army. Municipal positions became cosy jobs for former military officers and civil servants, people unconnected with the city and possessed of mediocre qualification and often suspicious conduct. The frame of mind of Wrocław's inhabitants was only improved in January 1742 when Frederic II granted Wrocław the status of a capital and residential city [Ratssiegel der Haupt- und Residenzstadt Breslau], thanks to which it became the third (after Berlin and Konigsberg) capital of Prussia. The King needed to have a castle here and to this end procured a property of the Episcopal Chancellor Gottfried von Spaetgen after the former's death by purchasing it from his heirs (the Chancellor had refused to sell it as long as he lived). Despite being partially devastated in later armed conflict, the building has survived to this day as the seat of the Municipal Museum.

While he was alive Frederic II frequently maintained that Silesia with Wrocław as its capital was the "pearl of the Prussian crown". Even so, he never went as far as securing a proper setting for his pearl, possibly due to his preoccupation with waging war. Indeed, between 1740 and 1763 Silesians enjoyed only seven years of peace. An economic revival of Wrocław took place at the end of the 18th Century and was accompanied soon after by demolition of the city's fortifications which had been stifling the city's expansion and provided scope for rapid urban development. The demolition of fortifications began in 1807 on the order of Jerome Bonaparte, brother of Napoleon, when the French army captured Wroclaw. The liquidation of fortifications opened the possibility for the city to merge with its outskirts: the Szweidnitz Outskirt, the Ohlau Outskirt, the Oder Outskirt and the Sand Outskirt. It also heralded the great construction boom of the 1850's.

Nineteenth-century Wrocław was a cosmopolitan metropolis. The harsh national divisions between Poles and Germans which were to cloud later history had not yet emerged, and German, Polish, French and Yiddish as well as Austrian dialects were widely spoken and understood. In 1826 a play by Karl von Holtei entitled *Der alte Feldherr* (1826) enjoyed great popularity. It was devoted to a Polish national hero and songs from the vaudeville were sang on the streets. Public opinion welcomed the outbreak of the November Uprising against Russia in 1830, while the insurgents of the January Uprising in 1863 were bolstered not only by Poles but also by Germans from Wrocław. "The entire city was full of conflicting information received from the Kingdom of Poland. Communication with the Kingdom has become so broken that neither train nor telegraph is able to cross the boarder and the fragmentary pieces of information which are getting through are undergoing

In January 1742 Frederick II granted Wrocław the status of a capital and residential city (Haupt- und Residenzstadt), thanks to which it became the third (after Berlin and Königsberg) capital of Prussia. Consequently, the King needed to have a royal residence here. He bought a palace (at present Kazimierza Wielkiego Street) from the heirs of Heinrich Gottfried Spaetgen and had it enlarged. (The Library of Frederick II, archival photograph from around 1930.)

In this palace King Frederick William III established in 1813 the highest German wartime order – the Iron Cross and signed the famous manifesto "An mein Volk" (To my nation), a call to arms against Napoleon (archival photograph from around 1930).

This historic house was erected in 1853 and continues to attract visitors' attention thanks to its rich decorations, especially the two-tier corner oriel with figures of St. John the Baptist, the patron saint of Wrocław and St. Jadwiga (St. Hedwig), the patron saint of Silesia. This is a highly intriguing ornament, particularly when we consider that the owner was of Jewish extraction (contemporary photograph).

The Salt Market – on the left a baroque historic house belonging to the Jewish Foundation of Heymann Oppenheim which ran care houses for the poor. Over the entrance there remains a decorative family initial. The adjacent house was the seat of a famous Wrocław pharmacy as early as the Middle Ages. Its emblem was a negro (Apotheke zum Scharzen Mohren). Modernist reconstruction of the building was carried out by Adolf Rading in 1928 (contemporary photograph).

wide and varied private interpretation." – reported a correspondent from "Czas" (Time), a Cracow newspaper, in Wrocław on 28th January 1863.

One Wrocław newspaper wrote of a sixteen year old man from a very good German family, that "he ran away with a Polish colleague, not taking a single coin from his home". A girl gained even greater publicity when she decided to play the role of an insurgent heroin and managed to match the fame of the adjutant to the general Marian Langiewicz, Henryka Pustowójtówna. As the "Breslauer Zeitung" reported in July 1863, the girl left behind a letter for her parents in which she wrote that she intended to make her way to the battle front disguised as a man and, even more shockingly, in male company. The newspaper went on to assure its readers that: "Her trail has already been discovered and one may safely anticipate that the young lady, cured of her illusions, will shortly be returned to her distressed family."

All the while the Jewish community continued to grow. In 1746, 534 Jews resided in Wrocław which accounted for not much more than 1 percent of all inhabitants of the city. By 1810 this figure had climbed to over 3250, approximately 5 percent of the city's population. The rate of population increase for Jews in the capital of Silesia was raising faster than anywhere else in Prussia. Jews were also becoming increasingly wealthier and better educated, enjoying success in trade, banking, industry, culture, science and politics. They were setting up foundations, opening schools and building temples. One of the grandest and most beautiful synagogues was erected on Wallstrasse (modern day Pawła Włodkowica street) which was known as the "Under the White Stork" Synagogue. This building survives to the present and still fulfils its original role as a house of worship as the only remaining synagogue in Wrocław.

The most famous Jewish institution in Wrocław was rabbinical school, which was opened in 1854 at 14 Wallstrasse (on the southern side of the present Pawła Włodkowica street; the building still existed in the 1960's). Studies with a specialisation in teaching/education lasted three years, whereas the course in Rabbinical studies lasted seven. Students had at their disposal a library which housed the largest collection of Jewish books in Europe including a unique collection of medieval manuscripts bought from Leon Vita Samuel of Trieste. During the War the collection was almost completely destroyed. Robert Gordis, the American Judaist, called the Wrocław seminary "the most famous institution for the education of rabbis in Europe" in Encyclopaedia Britannica. In 1939 723 students graduated the seminary.

IN THE CLUTCHES OF TOTALITARIANISM

In the 20th Century Wrocław and its inhabitants become the victims of two totalitarian regimes – the Nazis under Hitler and the Communists under Stalin. Over the course of this period the entire multinational and multicultural heritage of Wrocław was rejected and swept away. The fascist ideology of National Socialism was based on a strong sense of German nationalism which had became stronger at the end of the 19th Century, during the days of empire, and popular disillusionment arising from the acute economic, social and political problems prevalent in the German State after the First World War.

– I was six when Nazis came to power. Actually I do not remember anything of those times. Somehow politics avoided our home. But I remember the arrival of Hitler in Wrocław in March 1936 before consecutive elections to the Reichstag. He delivered a speech to thousands of supporters in the Jahrhunderthalle. Fortunately I did not have to listen to this – recounts Ingeborg Marinek, an inhabitant of the German Wrocław. – I also remember Kristallnacht ["the Crystal Night"] a pogrom against Jews instigated by the SS and taking place from 9th to 10th November 1938. I saw the biggest synagogue in Wrocław burning – Neue Synagoge [Synagoge Am Anger] at Angerstrasse [presently Łąkowa street]. I saw demolished stores. Glass from broken displays covered pavements in a thick layer. The next morning I went to school at Augustastrasse [presently Szczęśliwa, Pabianicka, Wesoła streets]. At the beginning I thought that I was witnessing a robbery. In the evening my father came back home and described how a rabbi from the Neue Synagoge dashed himself to the ground in despair because his temple was dying – recounts Ingeborg Marinek.

A controlled "anger of the people" was unleashed as the stores and private apartments of Jews were burned and demolished. The operation was carried out by uniformed SS-men. Walter Tusk, a Jewish trader, who on the morning of the 10th November left his house at Sadowastrasse [presently Stawowa street] encountered numerous vestiges of their activity. The Hirschlik bakery at Teichstrasse [presently Stawowa street] the ironmongers store belonging to Brauer & Sohn and a small confectionery company owned by Cheimowitz were all damaged. "Window-frames were cleaned of glass down to the smallest particles. The streets were covered with the contents of shop displays which had been unscrupulously looted and robbed. In a small pharmacy at Gartenstrasse [presently Piłsudskiego street], round the corner, everything had been thrown off the shelves and was laying on the floor. There were boxes and bowls lying everywhere" – wrote Walter Tausk.

By ten o'clock in the morning all Jewish stores in Wrocław, without exception, were demolished. Then the arrests commenced. Both eighty years old man and fourteen years old children were detained. Tausk mentioned in a dairy about arrest of a doctor, Nathan Salomschin, a sixty years old man, suffering from acute nephrocolic "He was kept on his legs for 11 hours along with about 500–600 arrested persons on both prison yards in the edifice of the Police Presidium. They were told to clasp hands for warm-up and walk in circles.

Hence, it was no wonder that many detainees died. "Just today I learned about a lethal heart attack suffered on the police station by the 66-years old Alfred Oschinsky, father of my acquaintance Arno. Until recently both of them had a superb furniture representation, founded about 40 years ago." – wrote Walter Tusk in his diary.

The police pulled Jews out of their apartments, arrested them on the streets and in hospitals. Doctors, assistants, male personnel and all patients able to walk from the Jewish hospital in the District of Krietern were transported to Buchenwald. Doctor Gradenwitz – one of the most popular doctors in Wrocław, a Christian – shot himself in full view of policemen. The Gestapo later turned up at his funeral and arrested one of the mourners – he was 75 years old.

Between the events of the Crystal Night and the last deportation of Wrocław Jews passed a period of just six years. Throughout this time transportswere sent to the notorious concentration camps at Maidanek, Trebling, Sobibór, Bełżec and above all to Auschwitz-Birkenau. In autumn 1944 one of the largest centres of German Jews, which at the turn of the century had numbered 20 thousand people, had ceased to exist.

Poles residing in Wrocław also became the object of Nazi hatred and brutality. The majority of parents became increasingly afraid to send their children to school. Rudolf Tauer started to attend a Wrocław Polish school in Wrocław in 1936 and recalls that the pupils never numbered more than twelve. He himself was of Polish-German extraction – his mother, Józefa Tulińska, was a Pole who originally came from Grodzisk Wielkopolski. She arrived in Wrocław from Poznan to take up a position as a housekeeper at a Jews' residence in 1922. She married George Tauer, an inhabitant of the city, six years later. Despite the fact that her own father was German she could neither speak nor understand the language, and he had expressed no objection to her imbuing her children with a strong sense of Polish identity. Later, when I had my own difficulties with Polish language my German father always encouraged me saying: "Learn it, because it may prove useful to you later" – recalls Rudolf Tauer.

– Following the outbreak of the War the situation of Wrocław's Polish inhabitants further deteriorated. When a Pole met his fellow citizen they were afraid to speak. From time to time we learned that this Pole had been arrested, and that another had been sent to Berlin and did not return – remembers Rudolf Tauer. – When the doorbell rang unexpectedly, my mother's first thought was always that it was somebody come to arrest us. We lived in constant fear. The Gestapo knew well, that my mother belonged to the Polish Association in Germany, that I attended Polish school and was a Polish scout. During the War my mother met Mrs. Günther, a Pole, who had married a German and who also belonged to the Association of Poles. She used to go to her place at eleven o'clock in the morning to listen programmes from London.

However, even in those difficult times people managed to get together and talk.

– Wartime Wrocław connected me with Günter. He was a little bit older than me, and stamp-collection brought us together – recounts Tauer. – We met by coincidence in 1940. I was collecting stamps and so was he. By this time my Polish origins had come to light. I had quite a few Polish pre-war stamps. Apart from that I received correspondence from an uncle interned in Romania. This was not a factor in my friendship with Günter though. We never quarrelled about who was right. We felt neither antagonism nor hatred. I think this is the privilege of those people who experienced the War while still in their youth. We understood that Good and Evil did not have nationalities. In 1944 my friend was drafted into the army and in May 1945 he found himself in the vicinity of Berlin. He was captured by the Soviets but managed to escape and took refuge in our house. After the War he established himself in Berlin, and started visiting us in Wrocław after 1965. We are still friends to this day.

The Neo-Gothic Church of St. Michael Archangel in Ołbin was the place of Edith Stein's prayers. She was a philosopher of Jewish origin. She was born in Wrocław in 1891, became a Carmelite nun in 1933 and was eventually murdered in the death camp in Auschwitz. Today she is revered as a Roman Catholic Saint. Her family's house was situated at 38 Michaelisstrasse (presently Nowowiejska Street). After her baptism in 1922, she visited the church every time she stayed in Wrocław (contemporary photograph).

The Synagogue on the Pasture (Synagoge Am Anger) was erected in 1872 according to a design by Edwin Oppler and was the second biggest synagogue in Germany (the largest was in Berlin). It had 1850 seats. It was destroyed during the Crystal Night in 1938 (archival photograph from 1929).

THE CITY BECOMES A FORTRESS

In 1945 the city lost its inhabitants twice. The first time as part of a dramatic exodus. In January 1945 all inhabitants of Wrocław had to leave the city at the command of Nazi Gauleiter, Karl Hanke. That winter was particularly bitter with the daytime temperature dropping as low as –16 C. A frosty wind cut through clothing with an icy bite which brought death to many an animal and many a person. Vast columns of frightened refugees filled the roads or made their pathless ways across country. In many places the living past piles of corpses lying by the wayside. On 19th January 1945, the Reich Defence Commissar ordered an immediate, compulsory evacuation of the city. Only able-bodied men capable of handling a rifle were permitted to stay behind. The callous decision to evict the civilian population in preparation for a long siege cost the lives of almost 100,000 people.

"The railway stations were jammed with people all day long and it was virtually impossible to fight one's way through the tightly pressed crowd. People were desperately trying to cram themselves and their belongings onto trains which were already full. The trains were only permitted to carry a limited number of evacuees while those unable to get on board must stay and try the next time – noted Wrocław priest Paul Peikert. And he went on to add: "Mothers with small children, pregnant women, the old and emaciated and struggling with a stick – fought frantically to gain purchase. That was the situation at the railway station in those days. The evacuees would wait for long hours, sometimes even a day or two, in the biting cold for permission to board a train for Germany. A women with four small children (the eldest aged eight years, the youngest eight days) lay for 36 hours at the Freiburger Station. Exhausted she later went home with her children because she was not allowed on the train. Sometimes mothers would go into premature labour brought on by the stress and hysteria around them. Children often became lost in the huge crowd. The names of lost children were announced but nobody came to claim them. I was also informed that at the Central Station 60–70 children were suffocated or trampled to death." To this day family members estranged in this way are still seeking to find one another. German television, ZDF, regularly shows pictures of people who last saw their loved ones over half a century ago and have no clue as to their whereabouts or fate.

Those unable to get out by train had to leave on foot. Gauleiter Hanke had this decision thrust upon her when loud speakers announced that women and children were to leave immediately, taking the direction of Opperau-Kanth. Luiza Hartmann did not know what to do. "It was inconceivable that her father would be able to make the journey. Hobbling on his false leg he probably would not even reach the highway. Luiza and her family then had to make the hardest decision they have ever made – her mother and sister would flee and try to reach their relatives in Dresden while Luiza would stay with her father in Wrocław. [...] Her mother and sister departed the next morning. Luiza never saw her mother again and what became of her may never be known for sure."

Frostbite, hunger and exhaustion all took their toll. The wake of the panic-stricken refugees was littered with the frozen bodies of infants and the elderly. The evacuees arrived in Neumarkt after a twenty kilometre march. The next day forty corpses had to be removed from the main square. The authorities urged the displaced after their tragic experiences by telling them to take etnas with them.

Despite brutal evacuation about 200,000 civilians stayed behind. There were also considerable numbers of prisoners of war and foreign compulsoryworkers, Poles among them, their situation deteriorating with each passing day. They were detained in camps, the biggest of which was located in present-day Hauke-Bosaka street. Over 10,000 people were send there including 2,000 Poles.

"People were crammed into all the rooms, in the corridors, bathrooms and under the stairs. Women, men, children. Infants and old men. Depressed,hopeless people. Several times a day the men and women were mobilised for a few shifts. Those who left for Kaiser-Strasse [to build a runway] were bid farewell as though they were going to certain death. The enemy bombardment commenced at 8 p.m. everyday. Most people did not return from this shift or else they were carried in the arms of their companions" – recounts Irena Siwicka, who on 23rd of January 1945 came to Wrocław with a column of prisoners from the Gross Wartenberg camp.

AMONG THE RUINS

On the night of 15th to16[th] February 1945 the Soviet Red Army closed its net on Wrocław and began a siege which was to last until 6th May. During this period the urban landscape of the city was gradually reduced to smoking ruins.

On 1st April, Easter Sunday, the worst bombardment of the siege commenced. It lasted throughout the day and into Monday by which time districts on both sides of the river were on fire – on the right bank as far as Na Grobli street (Weldendamm), through Traugutta street (Klosterstrasse) and down to Oławska (Ohlauer), Pokutnicza, the Neumarkt square and the Sand Island.

– The Soviets used not only explosives but incendiary devices which transformed the city into a sea of fire which burned night and filled the air with thick, permeating black fumes. Rudolf Tauer recalls that on Easter Sunday while at his parents' home a bomb landed on a house on Nabycińska Street. The bomb hit a house on Wachplatz. The falling walls trapped people – "How they screamed to get them out of there ! And there was neither a rescue team nor equipment to remove the debris. Inhabitants of the neighbourhood tried in vain to dig them out…Wrocław was turning into a ghost town – recalls Rudolf Tauer.

– Everybody wanted the War to be over but people were afraid of what would happen if the city surrendered. Women were particularly terrified of the Russians [their reputation having already proceeded them] and yet the chances of surviving in beleaguered Festung Breslau were growing slimmer with each passing day. On the 7th of March an work obligation was imposed on all men over 10 and women over 12 years of age. Inhabitants not holding an identity card could face a court-martial and even be sentenced to death. Try to imagine this work going on in the streets of the burning city, being under continuous fire and bombardment. There seemed only two alternatives: death by firing squad or death in the streets – explains Tauer.

The defence of Breslau went on, and all the while the field postal service persisted and somehow managed to maintain a relatively regular flow of mail. Correspondence continued to be delivered from the outside by aeroplane up until 31st March 1945 when the airport at Klein Gandau was captured by the Soviets. After this date letters still managed to get through to the city thanks to supply-containers dropped by aircraft. The only remaining newspaper – "Schlesische Tageszeitung", which from the 18th February 1945 was an official "Frontenzeitung der Festung Breslau" also continued to be published throughout this time.

After the War, one of the two transitory camps for the German population in Wrocław was arranged at the Freiburger Bahnhof (today's Świebodzki Railway Station). From there they were transported in cattle-trucks to one of the occupation zones in Germany (contemporary photograph).

The city waterworks were still operating at the beginning of March and until the middle of the month gas was available there, supplied via an underground pipeline from the city of Waldenburg but it was of small consequence. The fate of the city had already been sealed.

– The news that Hitler had committed suicide came first but shortly afterwards rumours began to circulate that the German Army in adjacent Czechoslovakia were about to launch a counter-offensive to brake the siege and liberate the city. Then people began to mutter that the Red Army was about to launch a final assault which could come at any day. Terror intertwined with hope. A gigantic tannoy installed at the Russian posts called upon the people to rise up and join the besiegers, that to fight on was futile – recalls Rudolf Tauer.

The act of capitulation was signed at the Soviet headquarters in a cellar of Villa Colonia at present 14 Rapackiego Street. After signing it General Herman Niehoff sought to return to the city to effect its surrender. General Wladimir Głuzdowski stated that he was the first prisoner of war.

"Once in full control, the occupying Soviets put the ruined city to the torch. […] Gangs of looters ran from street to street, ransacking the war-damaged houses, driving out the cowed inhabitants" – wrote historian Norman Davis. While Ingeborg Marinek recalls that "In the summer of 1945 one could seldom encounter a Pole. The city was administrated by the Russians, and it was not until Autumn that the first transports carrying Polish settlers started arriving."

LAST DAYS, FIRST DAYS

Over the next few years, from 1945–1947 German Breslau underwent transformation into Polish Wrocław. The postwar external boarders of Poland were decided upon by the "Big Three" (the USA, the Soviet Union and Great Britain). At the Potsdam conference Joseph Stalin forced his backing of the Polish western border along the courses of the rivers Oder and Neisse . The Allies agreed on the evacuation of the remaining German population in "an organised and humanitarian way". On 15th December 1944 in London, Winston Churchill categorically stated that only "the total expulsion of the Germans from the area to be acquired by Poland in the West and North. […] is the method which, so far as we have been able to see, will be the most satisfactory and lasting. There will be no mixture of populations to cause endless troubles. A clean sweep will be made." For the German citizens of Breslau this meant expulsion. The Polish Communist authorities, formed under the patronage of the Soviet Union and barely able to maintain their own structures, were unable to ensure the safety of those evicted, and although arbitrary acts of retribution against the departing Germans were officially forbidden they were frequently tolerated. "Incorporation of East German territories to Poland and the driving out of the local German population was considered by the majority of Poles to be a just punishment for the crimes committed during the German occupation of Poland. The mistreatment of Poles during the War years had ensured thatremaining Germans would find little sympathy. Thus the cases of Polish assistance for persecuted and discriminated should be all the more appreciated" – wrote a German historian Joachim Rogall. Meanwhile the loss of 47 percent of Polish territory (according to the pre-war boarders of 1938) to the Soviet Union, as announced by the Allies at the Yalta Conference, imbued Poles with a strong sense of their own moral entitlement to compensation.

The first trainload of German deportees was to leave Poland on 1st October 1945. The deportees were first transferred to transit centres at the Wrocław Freiburger Station and in Kohlfurt. They were only permitted to take with them that which they could carry and even this property was often stolen from them. They were then herded into cattle-trucks and sent to one of the Allied occupation zones in Germany. A German priest who witnessed the arrival of one such transport watched as the door of a cattle-truck was opened in Görlitz and ten corpses were removed. Many people displayed strong symptoms of shock and hysteria. Those Germans who were left behind in Wroclaw were frequently evicted from their property and forced to work without pay.

– In 1946 our whole tenement was inhabited by Poles. All our neighbours had left. Only the Rademacher family remained but they had already changed their surname to Kołodziej and I thought that they would stay in Wrocław forever. Our new neighbours were very nice. I particularly remember a young student and a policeman. We said "Good morning" to one another. There were no conflicts – recalls Ingeborg Marinek – I even took up with this policeman. Later, a workmate, Alfons, visited him with his girlfriend Marylka. They both wanted to learn German.

In Autumn 1946, Ingeborg's father , Erich Marinek, decided to leave Wrocław. He managed to qualify for a transport carrying the sick – We stayed behind. Father could only take one person and my mother did not want to leave me. The train departed from the Freiburger station. I received a food packet from our neighbour – the policeman – which I gave to my father for his journey. He went to Bad Hersfeld in Hesse where his sister lived. Then he moved to the vicinity of Frankfurt. Doctor Weisstein, a Wrocław barrister, who was appointed to a post in Hesse's local government after the War, helped him. My father mentioned that he was bringing him food. Weisstein reciprocated. He testified that during the war father had had nothing to do with the Nazi crimes – explains Ingeborg Marinek. It was only in 1957 that she herself left Wrocław never to return. Her most precious keepsake is a picture from the Wrocław apartment which was damaged by a Russian bayonet. Ingeborg continues to miss her hometown to this day.

The Panorama Racławicka, a work of Jan Styka and Wojciech Kossak, was exhibited in Lvov from 1894. The big painting represents the victorious first battle of the Kościuszko Insurrection. On the 4th April 1794 Polish troops defeated the Russian army at Racławice. Although the painting arrived in Wrocław in 1946 it was not displayed to public until 1983 due to concern about its anti-Russian sentiments it might evoke (contemporary photograph).

In the same wagons that the old inhabitants of Wroclaw were leaving Wrocław that the new ones were arriving. Ironically, they were called "repatriates", even though they had been expelled from their motherland and were arriving in a foreign city. The eastern territories of Poland, where they had previously lived, were incorporated into the Soviet Union. They had experienced the most severe adversities of war – genocide, political purges and banditry. They had spent three to four weeks in transit after which they were expected to start a new life in the ruins of an alien city. Józef Krotowicz having spent his childhood in Lvov was expelled in 1946. "Mother packed clothes in a wooden box, together with bedding, plates, pots and other household goods and items which might prove useful in the future: a wall clock which always struck a later hour than it showed; an iron grain-mill which my mother used for grinding the corn she grew (I remember she cooked a most wonderful and nutritious maize porridge). A few pictures of no real material value – they were just copies or oleographs but we were sentimentally attached to a picture of Jesus' heart, in front of which our whole family used to pray. Our parents sold most of our furniture for next to nothing, retaining only an old, narrow radio cabinet which we used as a trunk for storage. They also hung on to an old "Łucznik" bicycle dating from before the War which my father used to ride to work and which I later inherited from him. These objects we took with us.

"My Lvov ended on a platform – recalled Krystyna Bockenheim (her memoirs recorded by Stanisław Bockenheim) – not in the elegant station under a glass dome, which was the city's pride where passengers boarded and from where I used to set out with my parents bound for cities of Rymanów or Hrebenów on vacation, but on a concrete platform where animals and cargoes were loaded and unloaded. Beginning on 10th February 1941 our relatives were herded onto cattle-trucks and taken to Russia[2], often forever. I also had to leave together with my mother and grandmother, also in such a wagon and I also was never to return. The only difference was that I was sent in the opposite direction. Nobody expected that a journey of a few hundred kilometres would take eight days".

However, the displaced persons slowly found their place in the world. – In the first year after the war the life in Wrocław was far from easy. Thoughworking persons were received quite large rations of bread, sugar, noodles, and salty speck, in order to get other food products one had to walk on foot to a store on Jedności Narodowej Street [which was then called the Joseph Stalin Street], situated close to the intersection with Nowowiejska Street [former Michaelisstrasse], until the tramline no. 6 was started up – wrote Jadwiga Domagałowa in her memoirs. – Fortunately at the beginning of 1947 father obtained a goat and a hen brought from the far away Białystok region. In the Summer of 1947 I bought a few more hens. We kept them in a laundry for fear of thieves. After two years the goat was killed to make stew since by then we were able to buy milk from the mother of one of the professors of law (at that time still a student) who lived nearby. She kept two cows in a garage and everyday led them out to pasture on the bank of the river Oder.

The Krotowicze family settled in Wrocław on Struga Street (former Linnestrasse), on the first floor of a roofless tenement block. "Our life in this ruin left behind by Germans was not pleasant. The apartment was old, with old wallpaper infested with bedbugs which seemed determined to make our life uncomfortable. By

[2] Joseph Stalin, until 1941 allied with Adolf Hitler, pursued the policy of repression on the eastern territories of Poland occupied by the Red Army. Mass deportations of civil population, often whole families, to penal colonies or labour camps inside the Soviet Union were one of its instruments.

Wrocław was one of the most actively involved cities in the Solidarity movement. The city reacted to the declaration of martial law on the 13th December 1981 with mass demonstrations. The largest demonstration in Poland took place here on the 31st August 1982 when protesters numbered almost 50,000 people. During the protest one person was killed and 8 others were shot and wounded. Other mass demonstrations took place on the 1st May 1983. In the picture is a patriotic demonstration in Kościuszko Square.

The gnomes are the symbol of Orange Alternative (Pomarańczowa Alternatywa), Wrocław's happening movement of the mid to late 80s, which ridiculed the absurdity of communist reality. The first two gnomes were born on the night of 30th August 1982. They were created by Waldemar Frydrych (nicknamed Major, the head of the movement) and Wiesiek Cupała. The inhabitants of Wrocław saw them on walls throughout the city (a few of them were preserved up to now). During joyful street merry-making and parades of the gnomes the youths threw flowers instead of stones at the hostile militia officers (contemporary photograph).

night they used to emerge and bite us mercilessly. Water literally dripped from the ceilings and we had to position wash-bowls to capture the droplets otherwise it would have been impossible to live there."

To Krystyna Bockenheim "the new motherland seemed nothing but a sea of ruins. Some streets looked like ravines, because the roadway showed only tramlines and the rubble put aside was reached as high as the first floor of the burnt-out houses. [...] On our way we passed the more and less badly-damaged residences as well as churches and an edifice of the present-day University library which affronted the "Lvovian eye" with the redness of its clinker – we hadn't had anything like that where we'd come from and we found the Neogothic style quite repulsive".

THE LVOV LEGACY

But it was the very people, for whom Wrocław was so alien who were to leave a permanent imprint on the city. Most professors at the post-war University and Technical University came from Lvov. It was they who called the tune of the Silesian metropolis' life as well as the tramway-workers with whom inhabitants of Wrocław had the most frequent contact. People from Lvov usually arrived in organised groups and stuck together. They often keenly emphasised their origin and many companies used the adjective "Lvov" in their names and thus attracting customers who came from the same region as the proprietors.

In 1945 Józef Pitry opened "Lwowskie Piekiełko" (Lvov Hell) at Rydygiera street (former Gustav-Müller-Strasse), a restaurant with dancing. A German orchestra was played, and the recently opened Piastowski Brewery supplied beer, and also "Bar Lwowski" (Lvov Bar) and "Ta Joj" bar, but it was Fonsio who became the true king off the Wrocław catering trade.

"Fonsio reportedly used to run a popular non-alcoholic eatery in Lvov for indigent clientele. [...] It is always crowded here, because Fonsio caters very well and turns modest products into true dainties. Many University professors eat here. A display window is decorated with a plate featuring an artificial bunch of grapes. The sight of this quasi-decorative plate, brought here from Lvov, becomes less and less tempting with every passing month, but this does not deprive the customers of their appetites" – noted Joanna Konopińska on 11th November 1945.

Not only masters with ladles but also masters with scissors from Lvov lived and worked in Wrocław. "The Lvov Barber" located on present-day St. Matthew Square was popular (it was even featured on a postcard). In Wrocław the newspapers off the 1940's featured advertisements which emphasised the traders' and artisans' links with Lvov: "An older confectioner from Lvov will accept a good post, willing to travel" – advertised in the "Słowo Polskie" newspaper in 1948. "An inhabitant of Lvov is looking for an advisor in studies. I will pay a good rate for advice." – one could read such an ad in the Wrocław press in 1949.

Poles from the eastern border regions did not come to Wroclaw empty-handed and some of them brought with them authentic treasures many of which now form part of the collections of the Ossolineum Institute which had its first seat in Wrocław. The treasures deposited here came in two transports – one in July 1946 and the other in March 1947. In total there were 210,107 volumes including 6764 manuscripts and 42,606 old prints. The collections of the Ossolineum Institute contain, among other manuscripts, the works of the most eminent Polish romantic poets – „Pan Tadeusz" by Adam Mickiewicz and „Beniowski" by Juliusz Słowacki, as well as „Chłopi" („Peasants") – a novel for which Władysław Reymont received a Nobel prize in 1924 and „Zemsta" („Revenge") – a comedy by Aleksander Fredro, a monument to whom, also brought from Lvov, can now be found on Wrocław's Market Square.

The collection of graphics, wood engravings and drawings at the Ossolineum Institute constitute a real rarity and contain drawings by Rembrandt (inter alia *A Women with a child* and the Biblical scene *Tobiah and the angel*), Albrecht Dürer (*Head of a bearded old man*), Bartholomaeus Spranger (*Alegory of time and art*), Giovanni Antonio Pellegrini (*The Apostles*), Lorenzo di Credi (*The Beatifical Christ*). From among Polish artists the Ossolineum Institute houses the inter alia works of Jan Piotr Norblin, Cyprian Kamil Norwid, Aleksander Orłowski and Piotr Michałowski.

It took time for the newly settled people to put down roots in Wrocław, and in many cases decades. Throughout the Communist authorities, in an attempt to justify Polish claims to the city, distorted its history, placing emphasis on the period of Piast rule (whereby „Piast" became a synonym for „Polish") which alone was considered to be true heritage.

YOURS, OURS, MUTUAL

Only the fall of communistic regime and political transformation of 1989 enabled to reach to the multicultural heritage of Wrocław. Though generations of Poles born here after the war are not descendants of inhabitants living here before the war, they are still heirs of the cultural landscape and they take good care of it.

The decision made in 1990 by the Wrocław self-government to restore coat of arms granted to the city in 1530 by Emperor Charles V was a token of these changes. It is also worth remembering the energetic debate of 1999 when the Local assembly of the Lower Silesian Voivodeship decided on the coat of arms of the region, choosing a black Piast eagle against a golden background – a motif which had caused misgivings among some councillors because it might be suggestive of German affiliations.

The history of Wrocław and its culture is a strong foundation upon which one can build a sense of local identity and nourish openness and tolerance at the same time. And the inhabitants are able to take advantage of it. To that which was already in place here when they arrived, they have added that which they brought with them and this has enabled them to understand the history of their predecessors.

Agata Saraczyńska, granddaughter and daughter of Lvov inhabitants recalls that she knew the streets and side-streets of Lvov long before she visited them. "I used to take imaginary walks there with my great grandmother, I experienced the dramatic events of its defence [against Ukrainians in 1918] with my grandfather, a Lvov eagle. And although the older members of my family did not want to visit the city after the war, because – as they said – their hearts would break, in the days before "pierestroika" in Russia my father took us to visit his hometown. Thanks to this I can understand the sentiments of the former, German inhabitants of Breslau very well. It was not a tourist trip but a confrontation with the unreal. Not only did I visit the Bernadine Church and the Gothic Cathedral, the Orthodox Church of Wołoska and the Jura Cathedral, but we also walked the streets and looked in shop windows which no longer existed. We saw a school in which the hum of children was silenced, the place where a hill, so perfect for sledging, used to be. However, the thing I remember most of this sentimental journey is a Russian family, which expelled from St. Petersburg had settled in the abandoned house of my grandparents. They treated us with great hospitality, listening with the interest how their apartment used to be six times as big as it was now and how in the hall light filtered through stained-glass window and glittered on the marble floor. When, three years later, the granddaughter of Hans Schlicht visited my house in Wrocław which had been built so many years before by her grandfather, the time loop finally closed for me."

The German poet Heinz Winfried Sabais, born in Wrocław in 1922, wrote in a poem addressed to the Polish poet Tadeusz Różewicz:

Dear Tadeusz Różewicz !
We Are Cives Wratislavienses, God wanted it that way.
The city included both of us into its history.
Heraclitic Oder flows through your room and mine.
We have to like each other. Or else will die.

In 2001 a history of Silesia elaborated by Joachim Bahlcke was published in Germany, and because Germans have always spoken not of one Silesia but of two the book is entitled "Silesia and Silesians". One Silesia was the Silesian people who left and dispersed throughout various regions of Europe, while the second Silesia – the land on the both sides of Oder – lay unattainable behind the Iron curtain. And although the Iron Curtain has now been raised, Silesia still retains its double dimension to this day. Poles are learning to accept the multicultural past of the region and Germans the presence of Poles.

Beata Maciejewska

In 2000, eleven years after the beginning of political transformation and the recovery of independence (the last Soviet troops left Poland in 1993), the city joyfully celebrated its millennium i.e. the thousandth anniversary of the first written record of Wroclaw and the creation of a bishopric here. On 24th of June (St. John the Baptist's Day) a patriotic mass was celebrated in the Main Square to commemorate the bishopric and the city. The whole Polish Episcopate and church authorities from the neighbouring countries as well as the President and Prime Minister of the Republic of Poland were in attendance.

1. "I must say a few words about the City Hall which is, indeed, most admirably beautiful" wrote a 19th century Polish writer Józef Ignacy Kraszewski. In the picture: the eastern façade in late-Gothic style (end of the 15th century). In front of the City Hall is the pillory which has recently been renovated.

2. The astronomical clock was placed on the eastern façade in 1580. The hand of the sun sphere indicates hours whereas the hand of the moon sphere – moon phases. At the corners are ancient Egyptian symbols for the seasons.

3–4. Heinrich von Korn, Wrocław's publisher, collector and art patron, was portrayed in the sculpture of a burger which was mounted on the southern façade of the City Hall in 1891. His figure became part of "The Gallery of Townspeople". Alexander Kaumann, a construction adviser in the 19th century Wrocław was portrayed in the costume of … a medieval Alderman.

5. Fragments of the frieze in the southern façade date back to the 15th century. In the photograph: a vender being wheeled in a barrel.

6. Late Gothic carved ornaments on the southern façade of the City Hall excellently correspond to the 19th century "Gallery of Townspeople" i.e. a gallery of several statues under canopies. The figures were conceived by Karl Lüdecke who also supervised their construction.

7. The oriel in the western façade of the City Hall which dates from 1504.

8. The western façade of the City Hall adorned with a tower with a Renaissance cupola. In front of the City Hall, the monument of count Aleksander Fredro, the Polish writer of comedies, which stood in Lvov from 1897 to the end of the Second World War. At present one of the most popular monuments in Wrocław.

9. The interiors of an old chapel on the first floor with a vault supported by one pillar. Currently it houses museum and occasionally functions as a small-audience concert hall. On the right is the portal over the entrance to the Grand Hall, on the left, the portal over the entrance to the old Chamber of the City Council Senior.

10. The Grand Hall of the City Hall, the middle nave. The portal which dates from about 1485 is adorned with coats of arms featuring the Czech lion, Silesian eagle and the bust of John the Evangelist, patron saint of the chapel in the City Hall. It is also evidence of Wrocław's dependence on the Czech Crown.

11–12. The middle oriel of the Grand Hall is decorated with sculpture dating from the turn of the 15th century. The entrance is marked symmetrically with figures of knights and monkeys. Due to the floor, which was higher than in the hall, the oriel fulfilled the role of the loge of honour from which one could observe the celebrations and festivities being held there.

13. The western part of the Main Square was already known as the Wool Market in the Middle Ages, and wool continued to be traded here until 1905 and few people were surprised by the presence of heaps of sacks. The western frontage of the Main Square is marked on the left with a "tower block" which was finished in 1931 as the former Municipal Savings Bank (currently WBK Zachodni Bank)

14. The northern side of the Main Square is known as the Vegetable Market or Delicacies' Market Side. In the background is a tower of St. Elisabeth's Church, one of two parish churches of the late Middle Ages.

15. The Merchant's House formerly belonging to the brothers Arthur and George Barasch (today's "Feniks" department store) is built into the eastern frontage of the Main Square. The art nouveau building was crowned with a lit crystal globe with the diameter of 6.5 m which was destroyed in 1929 by lightning.

16. The Glass Fountain, built in the western part of the Main Square to the design of the Wrocław sculptor Alojzy Gryt is called "Zdrój" (the spring) after the name of the former Mayor of Wrocław (1990–2001), Bogdan Zdrojewski. He was an ardent advocate of the controversial form of the fountain.

17. The southwestern part of the Main Square with the monument to Aleksander Fredro in the foreground. The area is a popular meeting point for courting couples and the site of political demonstrations.

18. The historic houses, nowadays called Jaś i Małgosia (Hensel and Gretchen) were formerly the homes of altar service members of the adjacent St. Elisabeth's Church. Jaś (the smaller one) dates from the Renaissance period, whereas Małgosia dates from the Baroque. They are connected by a baroque gate bearing the inscription "Mors Ianua Vitae" (Death – a gate to life) and which once led to a church burial ground.

19. St. Elisabeth's Church (which holds the title of basilica) has functioned as a parish church since 1245. In 1999 a monument (by Karl Biedermann) was erected in the square adjacent to the church. The monument commemorates Dietrich Bonhoeffer, an inhabitant of Wrocław, born in 1906, and Protestant theologian who was involved in an ecumenical and anti-Nazi movement. He was executed in the Flossenburg concentration camp in 1945.

20. St. Elisabeth's Church, apart from fulfilling religious functions (Roman Catholic military and civil parish church), is also the venue for concerts. Until the great fire of 1976 the church housed the most magnificent organs in Silesia which dated from the 18th century and were the work of Michael Engler Jr.

21. St. Elisabeth's Church had strong historical ties with Poland, especially in the 16th and 17th centuries. Its clergymen were known for their merits for the presence of the Polish language in Evangelical services in Silesia (Jan Akolut, among others)

22. St. Elisabeth's Church is a mausoleum for the most affluent burgher families of Wrocław. Many of the people buried here chose to live in Wrocław having arrived in the city from Saxony, Bavaria, Hungary and Poland. The main element of the epitaph (from 1585) of Nicklas Rehdiger, patrician and city councillor, are figures of his family members, men and women, kneeling opposite each other (in the photograph: close-up).

23. The tomb monument of Johann Georg von Wolff (from 1722), the Emperor's adviser and senator, was executed according to a design by Joseph Emmanuel Fischer von Erlach. The sculpture composition (7.5 m high) is deeply symbolic.

24. The mannerist tombstone, erected by the patrician Heinrich Rybisch (to commemorate himself) in St. Elisabeth's Church, was considered a manifestation of pride in the 16th century Wrocław, the inhabitants of which smeared it with axel grease.

25. The view from the tower of St. Elisabeth's Church overlooking Ostrów Tumski (Tumski Island) and Wyspa Piaskowa (Sand Island). On the right, in the background is the cathedral. On the left: the dark silhouette of the Church of Our Lady, and in front of it a lit building of the former monastery of Canons Regulars (currently the University Library). In the background can be seen the tower and Church of the Holy Cross.

26. The view from the tower of St. Elisabeth's Church towards the West i.e. the former Mikołajskie Suburbs incorporated into the city after the demolition of its fortifications in 1807 at the command of Jerôme Bonaparte, brother of Napoleon.

27. The present-day Kiełbaśnicza Street dates back to the foundation lay-out of 1242. On the corner of today's Łazienna Street is the Gothic and Renaissance historic building of George Baumann's printing-house where, starting from 1632, the first newspaper of Wrocław was printed.

28. The present-day Jatki, the passage existing already in 1266, was then famous for its butchers' stands. In the course of time butchers were replaced by artists. Today only bronze monuments of animals serve as a reminder of the street's past.

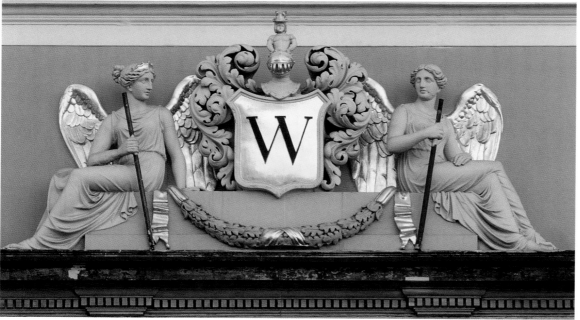

29–30. The Old Exchange in the Salt Market was erected between 1822 and 1825. The exchange room in the building was occasionally used as a ball-room. In the building there were also other rooms serving presentation functions. Architect Karl Ferdinand Langhans gave the exchange the character of an Italian municipal palace of the Renaissance period.

31. In the Salt Market dating from the time when the Main Square was delineated, not only salt was sold here but also honey, leather, ropes and goat's meat. The square was also called the Polish Square due to the fact that many of the merchants there were Polish.

32. The view from the Main Square overlooking the Salt Market. The southern side of the Main Square was called the side of Golden Cup (named after the emblem of one of the historic houses). In the middle of the 19th century it housed the renowned Immerwahr's store, selling fashionable clothes from Paris, that often attracted Poles passing through Wrocław.

33. The Church of St. Mary Magdalene was the second parish church of the medieval city (the Church of St. Elisabeth being the first one). In the days of the Reformation Johannes Hess, a friend of Martin Luther and Philipp Melanchton, was a parish priest here. He was a Catholic and Evangelical clergyman, reformer of Wrocław who originally came from Nuremberg.

34. The tombstone of the syndic and imperial adviser Caspar Artzat (dated from 1679) is located in the Church of St. Mary Magdalene and was made by the Tyrolian artist Mathias Rauchmiller who was active at the Emperor's court in Vienna.

35. The Sacrament-house of the church of St. Mary Magdalene dating back to the end of the 14th century shows scenes of Christ's Passion: Flogging, Crucifixion and Resurrection (in the photograph).

36. The Romanesque portal (12th century) originating from the Benedictine Abbey (taken to pieces in 1529) in Ołbin (German Elbing) was built in the external walls of St. Mary Magdalene's Church in 1546. It is one of the most beautiful portals in Central Europe. Figural motifs represent the scenes from the lives of the Holy Virgin and Jesus Christ.

37. The shrine of three nations under the protection of St. Stanislaus, the patron saint of Poland, St. Wenceslas, the patron saint of the Czech Crown and St. Dorothy, the patron saint of German settlers. The monastic church of the Augustinians Eremites (later Franciscans) was founded in 1351 by Emperor Charles IV during his visit to Wrocław, forms material evidence of the city's multi-cultural past.

38. Baron Heinrich Gottfried von Spaetgen was a secretary at the court of Emperor Charles VI. He had a beautiful palace in Wrocław, which later became a residence of the Prussian kings. His tombstone in St. Dorothy's Church, executed by Franz Joseph Mangoldt, reflects the social status of the baron. The photograph shows a close-up of a symbolic figure on the tombstone: Chronos, personification of time and eternity.

39. Here in 1267 there was a cemetery chapel of Mary of Egypt, belonging to the parish of St. Mary Magdalene. The church was erected in its present form at the beginning of the 15th century, and was soon dedicated to St. Christopher. Between 1416–1829 Polish sermons were delivered here and a Polish school functioned at the church. Presently this Evangelical Church is the seat of a German-speaking Parish.

40. The Church of St. Christopher was enlarged in the Renaissance period. In the photograph: a close-up of the tombstone built into the northern wall of the church.

41–42. The Boulevard on Sand Island, surrounding the Church of Our Lady and the building of a former monastery of Canons Regular, is named after Piotr Włostowic (Peter Wlast), the founder of the original church and monastery of the 12th century. He was the most eminent personality in medieval Wrocław. Members of the association of the Dunin family regard themselves as his descendants.

Across the Odra River is the panorama of Tumski Island with the towers of the Cathedral of St. John the Baptist (on the right) and the Church of the Holy Cross (on the left).

43. "From the other bank, I shall remember the light of lanterns. / A splendid sight reflected on the river" – wrote the German theologian Joachim Konrad in a poem about Tumski Island.

44. A view from Kapitulna Street overlooking the Cathedral of St. John the Baptist; the baroque chapel of Resurrection in the background.

45. The Tumski Bridge (Pons Cathedralis) leading from Sand Island to Tumski Island once formed a border beyond which ecclesiastical jurisdiction was in force. From 1504 up to 1810 the municipal court could not prosecute criminals who crossed the bridge.

46. In Gothic and Renaissance building of the Chapter (beginning of the 16th century), in the vicinity of the Cathedral, the archives and library of the diocese were kept to the end of the 19th century. Currently the building forms part of the Archdiocesan Museum.

47. The Arcade which joins the Church of St. Giles on Tumski Island (the oldest preserved church in Wrocław) with the building of the Chapter (on the left) is called the noodle gate. According to the legend, the stone noodle on the arcade is the trace of a great love – here the ghost of a wife fed her husband delicious Silesian noodles. The baroque chapel called the Electoral chapel of the Cathedral is shown in the background.

48. St. Mary's statue in front of St. John the Baptist's Cathedral stood there in 1694 on the Cathedral Chapter's initiative. The Holy Virgin with the Child crushing the head of a snake that wreathes itself round the globe is called Maria Immaculata, victress over sin.

49. The Cathedral's 15th century western portico was rebuilt in the 19th century. However, many elements of the old decorations were preserved. In the niches: stone statues of St. Gregory the Great and St. Paul.

50. The figure of St. Jadwiga (St. Hedwig) of the cathedral's western portico. This saint came from Andechs in Bavaria and was a wife of Henry the Bearded, Piast Duke of Silesia. In her left hand she holds the miniature of the Cistercian church in Trzebnica (she was its founder), in her right hand – the figure of the Holy Virgin she never parted with.

51. A view of the Cathedral from the East. The two baroque chapels: St. Elisabeth's (on the left) and Electoral (on the right) are accompanied by the Gothic chapel of St. Mary (in the middle). The neo-Gothic towers are surmounted by cupolas built as late as 1991 (the old ones having been destroyed during the War) and mounted by means of a helicopter.

52. The cathedral's crypt exhibits the stone relics (dated from the 10th – 12th centuries) of the earlier buildings which stood in that place. The present-day shrine was constructed in stages from the 13th century onwards.

53. The Cathedral's nave and presbytery dating from the 13th century are shown in the background. During the *Festung Breslau* siege, the Cathedral was so badly damaged that many doubted whether reconstruction would be possible. However, work on reconstruction began in autumn 1946 and 5 years later the new cathedral, then called the *mother of Silesian churches*, was consecrated by the Polish Primate cardinal Stefan Wyszyński.

54–55. St. Elisabeth's Chapel (from Thuringia) in the cathedral was founded between 1680–1700 by Friedrich von Hessen, Landgrave of Hesse (bishop of Wrocław from 1671) who was eventually buried here. His tombstone (both a close-up and a general view of which are shown in the photographs) was made by Domenico Guidi. The patron of the chapel is the bishop's ancestress.

56. A view from the Cathedral's tower. On the right stands the Church of the Holy Cross, in the middle, Sand Island with the Church of Our Lady and the former monastery of Cannon Regulars (currently the University Library). On the left, in the background, are the silhouettes of the churches situated in the neighbourhood of the Main Square: St. Elisabeth's Church and St. Mary Magdalene's Church.

57. A view from the tower of the Church of the Holy Cross overlooking the cathedral. The oldest part of the city was situated here, on Tumski Island. Most probably it was built by the Czech at the beginning of the 10th century.

58. St. Martin's Church, the chapel of the medieval city on Tumski Island. It was built in the 13th century and has changed little since. Between the Wars the church was a shrine of the Polish community in Wrocław and their asylum. Between 1921–1939 sermons here were delivered in Polish. In the background stands the Church of the Holy Cross.

59. The Church of the Holy Cross was founded in 1288 by Duke Henry IV the Righteous to celebrate his reconciliation with bishop Tomasz II (Thomas II) and was intended to be the necropolis of Wrocław's Piasts. It has a reputation for being the most beautiful Gothic church in Wrocław.

60–61. The Botanical Gardens were established during the period 1811–16, as a university institution in the place of former fortifications. The remaining fragment of a moat is now a small pond. The Gardens house the University Museum of Natural History (formerly the Zoological Museum).

62. "It is due to the Jesuits that we have that old and beautiful building of thick walls and of deep window niches with the richly ornamented baroque »Aula Leopoldina«» and the »Concert Hall«" wrote Edith Stein, the later patron saint of Europe, about the university in 1911. In the photograph, the university building, the view from the tower of St. Elisabeth's Church. The Church of the Holy Name of Jesus in the background.

63. Jesuit Leopold University of Wrocław was established due to the donation of the castle by the Odra River to the Jesuits by Emperor Leopold I. The University opened in 1702 and a new baroque building was erected in the years 1728–43.

64–65. Four allegorical figures, symbols of the four university faculties, were put on the balcony balustrade of the Mathematics' Tower of the University in 1733. Theology and Law are shown in the photographs.

66. The main university entrance is decorated with a balcony portico with allegorical statues symbolising The Four Cardinal Virtues. Justice wields a sword.

67. University Concert Hall, formerly the Oratorium Marianum, was destroyed in 1945. As late as 1997 it was reopened to public after reconstruction which was made possible due to the photographic records from 1944 preserved in the Herder Institute in Marburg.

68–70. Aula Leopoldina, a splendid baroque hall where the architecture, painting and sculpture form a homogenous unity. Over the podium stands the apotheosis of Emperor Leopold II, the founder of the University. The figures of a bearded thinker with an ardent heart (in the photograph) and a woman with a beehive (representing Discernment and Diligence) accompany Leopold personifying the Emperor's motto *Consilio et Industria*. Below are the spurned figures of a woman with tousled hair (in the photograph) and a boy with donkey's ears (representing Discord and Stupidity).

71–72. The Jesuit Church of the Holy Name of Jesus is one of the most beautiful baroque interiors in Silesia. The magnificent paintings were created by Johann Michael Rottmayer, the founder of the Austrian Baroque Painting School. The church's dynamic and sculpture interior decorations were the result of a thorough reconstruction carried out from 1722 onward by the extraordinary architect and artist Jesuit Christophorus Tausch.

73–74. The former monastery of Crusaders with a Red Star was one of the biggest baroque projects in Wrocław. In 1810 the Catholic St. Matthias' Gymnasium was based here. After the Second World War the monastery became the seat of the Zakład Narodowy im. Ossolińskich (the Ossolineum Institute), moved here from Lvov, which houses many treasures of Polish culture. In the courtyard, regarded as a 'magical place', stands a beautiful baroque well.

75–76. The building of the former Province Management was finished in 1886. Currently it houses the National Museum (former Silesian Museum) with the saved collections of two other city museums which were destroyed during the Second World War: The Silesian Museum of Artistic Handicraft and Ancient Times and The Silesian Museum of Fine Arts. It also houses a collection of Polish art (from 17th to 19th centuries) originating from Lvov and Vilnius as well as Poland's biggest collection of Polish modern art.

77. Jaxa's (Peter Wlast's son-in-law) foundation tympanum from the monastery Church of St. Michael Archangel in Ołbin dated back to 1150–1163. Ołbin was in the 12th century the most densely inhabited district in the city and within the abbey there were as many as 3 churches. The tympanum and other relics of Romanesque art are currently exhibited in the Architecture Museum (in today's Bernardyńska Street).

78. A cloister garth in a museum? Yes. The Architecture Museum is based in the post-Bernardine Monastery, therefore it has its cloister garth. The monastery buildings, erected in the 15th and 16th centuries, were largely destroyed in 1945. Reconstruction was carried out according to a design of Edward Małachowicz from 1956 to 1974.

79. The Mikołajski Arsenal (in the present-day Antoni Cieszyński Street) shows that Wrocław was once a fortress. In the past, food and arms were stored here. Today it plays home to the museum exhibits and archival materials that are stored here. The buildings house a department of the Municipal Museum (with the biggest collection of helmets in Poland), the Construction Archives which is the department of the Architecture Museum.

80. St. Adalbert's Church originally served the first municipal parish. It is situated by the primaeval route North-South, leading through a historical crossing of the Odra River (through Sand Island and Tumski Island). In the photograph is shown a close-up of the 12th century frieze on the southern façade.

81. In 1226 St. Adalbert's Church was taken over by the Dominicans who arrived from Kraków under the leadership of Czesław Odrowąż. During the Mongol Invasion in 1241 he took refuge on Tumski Island and the townspeople believed that the city was miraculously saved thanks to his prayers. The baroque chapel, erected over the period 1711–1730, houses the alabaster sarcophagus of the blessed Czesław.

82. The baroque Church of the Holy Trinity (Traugutta Street), with perfectly preserved interiors, belongs to the Brothers of St. John of God order (Bonifratrzy), who arrived in Wrocław in 1711. Traditionally they have specialized in phytotherapy. During *Festung Breslau*, in the crypt of the church there was a clandestine hospital in which Father Doroteusz Heynoł, provincial of the order, sheltered more than a hundred Soviet and American prisoners of war.

83–84. The Church of God's Providence was raised between 1746 and 1759 as the court church on the initiative of Frederick II, the King of Prussia. Nowadays it is the main shrine of the Evangelical-Lutheran Church in the diocese of Wrocław. It is one of four churches (next to the Synagogue, Orthodox Church and the Catholic Church of St. Nicolas) situated in the neighbourhood as part of the so-designated District of Mutual Respect.

85. Fortunately, the White Stork Synagogue was not damaged by the Nazis. It is an outstanding example of Classicism designed by Karl Ferdinand Langhans. The Jewish community, once numerous and affluent, was exterminated during the Second World War. Now, the synagogue is owned by the present small Jewish community. It is one of the four shrines in the District of Mutual Respect. In the photograph is the interior of the synagogue during a theatrical play, one of events organized to celebrate 800-year anniversary of the Jewish Community in Wrocław (October 2003)

86. The cemetery chapel of St. Elisabeth's parish was erected here (today's Św. Mikołaja Street) at the end of 13th century. St. Barbara's Church took its Gothic shape at the end of the 15th century. Since 1963 it has been an Orthodox church which cooperates with churches of other denominations in the District of Mutual Respect. In the photograph is the iconostasis in the sacristy of the church.

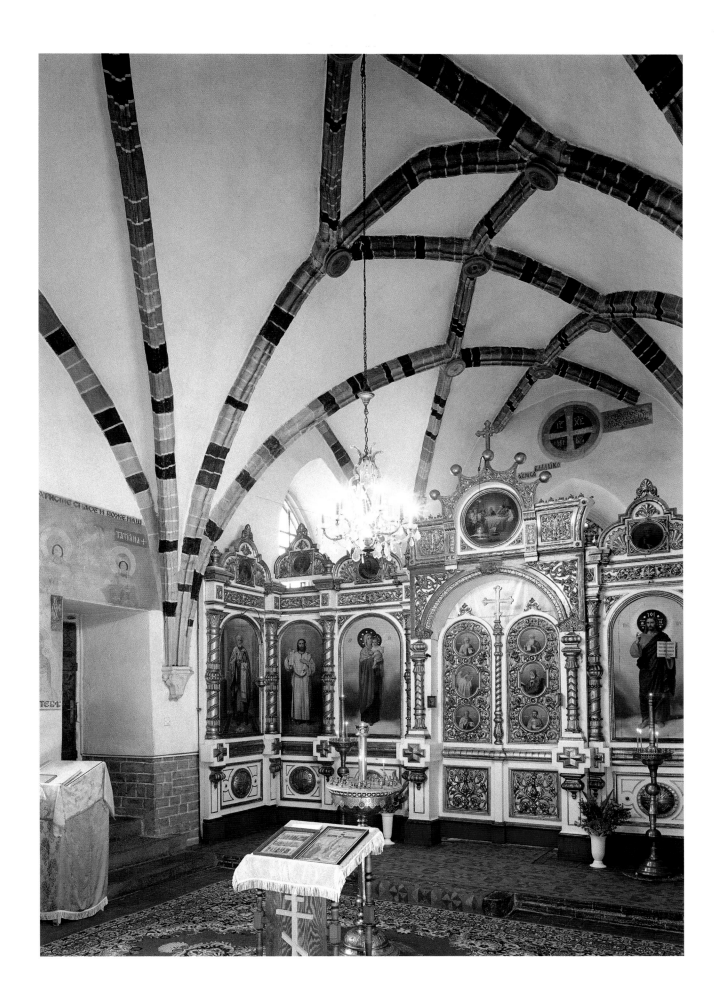

87. St. Maurice's Church (today's Traugutta Street), mentioned in the records as early as 1234, was surrounded by a Valon settlement in the Middle Ages. The baroque tower was erected in 1723. The church took the present-day form during the reconstruction at the end of 19th century. The last German parish priest of St. Maurice's parish, Reverend Paul Peikert was the author of a terryfying chronicle of the *Festung Breslau* siege. The reconstruction of the church, which was 60% destroyed in the fighting, was completed in 1967.

88. The classicistic epitaph of the Fryderyk Jakub and Ksawera Psarskis was built in the southern wall of St. Maurice's Church in 1806.

89–91. The University Library (today's K. Szajnochy Street) is housed in the 19th century building of a former Municipal Library. Before the Second World War the whole library collection was located in a former monastery building on Sand Island (at present only the special collection of the library is kept there). During the War the most precious part of the collection was evacuated. The volumes which remained in Wrocław (approx. 500,000) were burnt on the night of 9th May 1945. Apart from the general collection, the library possesses a unique collection of manuscripts, old prints, graphic and cartographic collection connected with the history of Silesia.

92. The palace erected in the years 1785–87 (K. Szajnochy Street) for Gideon von Pachaly, the main tax collector in the War and Domain Chamber, designed by Karl Gotthard Langhans. The building now belongs to the University Library.

93. The building of the former municipal baths (today's Curie-Skłodowskiej Street) constructed according to a design by Max Berg during the period 1912–14. Apart from the baths, it also housed the Revenue Office and a shelter for single mothers.

94. In the water-tower in the present-day Na Grobli Street one can see the unique 18-metre high steel construction of a pumping-steam machine dating from 1879 (designed by Thometzk, an engineer). Nowadays the water-tower building functions as a museum and a stage for theatrical performances.

95. The wooden Przedtumski bridge was a part of a historical crossing of the Odra River. In 1885 a steel construction called the Gneisenau Bridge was erected there. Today the bridge is called "Młyński" (The Mill Bridge) and connects St. Jadwiga Street with the present-day Bema Square.

96. The 19th century Zwierzyniecki Bridge (formerly "Passbrücke"), located in the western part of the city, is supported by four columns of red sandstone. It is adorned with low reliefs featuring motifs from Wrocław's coat of arms.

97. Wrocław's most famous bridge, has been called the Grunwaldzki Bridge since 1947 (before the War it was known as the Emperor's Bridge). It used to be the second largest suspension bridge in Germany. Emperor Wilhelm (William) II himself was present at the opening ceremony in 1910.

98. The former department store at today's 32 Rzeźnicza Street was opened in 1901. The building belonged to the Schlesinger & Grünbaum company which dealt in the wholesale of ready-made clothing for men and boys. The company ceased to operate due to persecution of Jews before 1939.

99. The decision to build the Royal Higher Technical School was taken in 1902. The block of school buildings (today the Technical University of Wrocław) was erected in a few stages from 1905 onwards. In the photograph is the entrance (Norwida Street) to the main building, built in the first stage of construction. The sculpture designed by Richard Schipke.

100. The present-day main building of the Technical University of Wrocław in Wybrzeże Wyspiańskiego Street was erected as late as 1925–28. It was designed by Max Schrimer and Heinrich Müller.

101. The machine laboratory of the Royal Higher Technical School (in the present-day Smoluchowskiego Street) was created in the first stage of the construction of the block between 1905–10.

102–103. The Hundred Years' Hall, situated in the vicinity of the Szczytnicki Park, in the eastern part of the city, was erected in 1913 to celebrate a hundredth anniversary of the war to liberate Prussia from Napoleon's army. The investment was financed from the municipal coffers, some councilors protested, saying that the money should not be wasted on a building resembling 'a gas container' or 'a hat-box.'

104. The Hall, presently called the People's Hall, is a work of Max Berg, the eminent architect. Enthusiasts compared in to Babylonian ziggurats and the Hagia Sophia church in Constantinopolis. A water pool surrounded by a pergola (designed by Hans Poelzig) is located next to the Hall, on the side of the Szczytnicki Park.

105. The building was one of the first buildings created for the so-called "mass recipient." The Hall is the place of theatrical performances, musical concerts (once the Hall housed the biggest organs in the city), pre-election meetings, sporting events, religious gatherings (in 1997 the pope John Paul II prayed here) and even opera stagings. In the photograph is the premiere of Giuseppe Verdi's "Nabucco", prepared by the troupe of Wrocław's Opera.

106. At the time of opening in 1913 the Hundred Years' Hall was admired as the biggest ferro-concrete construction in the world. The dimensions of the Hall are also impressive – the diameter of the dome amounts to 65 m (over 20 m more than the Roman Pantheon) and the height – to 42 m.

107. The former exhibition pavilion, so called Pavilion of Four Domes (designed by Hans Poelzig), the seat of the Historical Exhibition of 1913. In 1952 it became the seat of the Feature Film Company. The first film – a crime story – was shot a year later.

108. The bird's-eye view shows the Hall and the Pavilion of Four Domes (on the left). Iglica (the needle-shaped construction) designed by Stanisław Hempel, situated in front of the Hall, has remained there after the Exhibition of Recovered Territory (held in 1948).

109. The 16th century Church of St. John Nepomuk has been located in the Szczytnicki Park since 1913. Together with a rural cemetery it was one of the exhibitions on the Exhibition of Cemetery Art, accompanying the Century Exhibition. The church was originally built in Stare Koźle in the Upper Silesia. Moving the church to Wrocław saved it from demolition.

110. The Szczytnicki Park (named after an old village of Alt-Schietnig) became a municipal property as late as in the second half of the 19th century. Beforehand, at the end of the 18th century, the English-style park was created here by the duke Friedrich Ludwig von Hohenlohe-Ingelfingen who made it available to inhabitants of Wrocław as the first open park in the city.

111. The Japanese Garden in the Szczytnicki Park was opened on the occasion of the Century Exhibition in 1913 as one of the exhibits of the Exhibition of Garden Art. In 1997 it was thoroughly renovated.

112. This house attracts architects from all over the world. It was designed by Hans Scharoun for single people and childless couples. Enthusiasts wrote that it looked like a ship anchored in port. This exemplary building (in today's Kopernika Street, in the vicinity of the Szczytnicki Park) was an element of the WuWA "Wohnung und Werkraum" (Flat and Workplace) exhibition of 1929.

113. The first modern department store in Wrocław (former Petersdorff, presently "Kameleon" department store in the present-day Szewska Street) erected in 1929 to an expressive design of Erich Mendelsohn. Even today it is admired for the elegance of its avant-guard shape. It reminds us that it is trade that has always made Wrocław go round.

114. The house once owned by architect Ernst May (currently in Moniuszki Street) is a typical example of modest and functional architecture designed by this eminent German architect and town planner, working in Wrocław from the First World War to 1925.

115. The housing estate of semi-detached houses in Ołtaszyn (in today's Strączkowa Street), designed by Ernst May, built between 1921 and 1922 for farm workers. A modern, yet modest social scheme was combined here with a kind of rural house surrounded by a garden.

116. The main square of the Karłowice housing estate embodying the idea of a city-garden. It became part of Wrocław as late as in 1928 as a luxurious villa district.

117. Tadeusz Kościuszko Square (formerly the square of Prussian general Friedrich Bogislav von Tauentzien). His monument, located in the centre of the square till 1945, was placed there in 1795, where the square itself did not exist. It was delineated in 1807, after pulling down the fortifications. Only few buildings in the square remained after the Second World War, including the building on the left, the biggest department store in the city, from 1928 the property of the Wertheim company (nowadays "Renoma" department store)

118. The Olympic Stadium, originally called Silesian, was created together with a recreation complex constructed between 1925–39 in the vicinity of the Szczytnicki Park. Richard Konwiarz was awarded a silver Olympic medal for the design of the stadium at the architectural contest of the Olympics in Los Angeles in 1932.

119. A bird's-eye view, on the left is an axel of the Bridge of Peace, on the right is an axel of the Grunwaldzki Bridge and Grunwaldzki Square, created as a result of planned burning and demolition of a compact development to build an airport (the action started on 7 March 1945). It is estimated that during this action, carried out at the time of Soviet bombardment, several thousand people lost their lives. These were prisoners of war and forced labourers of different nations (Poles included) as well as Wrocław's civilians.

120. The Southern Park was created in the years 1891–92 thanks to the initiative of Julius Schottländer, the owner of parts of Borek and Partynice, southern districts of the city. In return for including them into a municipal gas network, Schottländer offered 20 ha to the city (between present-day Ślężna Street and Powstańców Śląskich Street) to be used as a municipal park.

121. The Jewish cemetery in Ślężna Street, nowadays a section of the Municipal Museum, is the only preserved 19th century cemetery in Wrocław. The first funeral took place on 17 November 1856 and the cemetery started to take the present-day form at the end of the 19th century.

122–124. Tombstones, tomb monuments and tombs of the Jewish cemetery were created in various periods (also tomb plates, which are older than the cemetery itself and which were found in the city area, are exhibited here), hence the variety of styles and tastes. But they incorporate many common symbols e.g. hands in gesture of blessing symbolise a descendant of a high-priest, whereas an hourglass with winds denotes passing time.

125. The Cemetery of Russian Army Officers (in Karkonoska Avenue), who lost their lives during the siege of the city in 1945, has the shape designed for it by Tadeusz Ptaszycki in 1947. The monument of the soldiers, a monumental gloriette, was designed by Roman Feliński, first working in Lvov and then in Warsaw.

126. The Cemetery of Italian Soldiers (in Grabiszyńska Street) was consecrated in 1928. Mainly prisoners of war from the times of the First World War, who died in Silesia between 1915–18, are buried here. The Italian state financed the construction of the cemetery.

Rhapsodie Brahms.

Raphael Maszkowski
Dirigent des Breslauer
Orchester Vereins
geb. zu Lemberg am 11. Juli 1838
gest. zu Breslau am 14. März 1901.

127. The angel playing the violin has been part of the Grabiszyński cemetery for over a hundred years. It is a decoration of the tomb of Rafael Maszkowski, an eminent Polish artist from Lvov, a conductor of Breslauer Orchester Verein.

128. This tomb monument (1903) of high artistic value is one of the few old monuments preserved in the Grabiszyński cemetery.

129–130. In recent years the number of Wrocław's students increased twofold (to almost 130,000). The photograph shows new buildings of the Law and Administration Faculty at the University of Wrocław, in Kuźnicza Street (designed by Zbigniew Maćków and the team) and in Więzienna Street (designed by Ewa Frankiewicz).

131. The change of a political and economic system in 1989 brought about, among others, fast economic development. Today Wrocław is the seat of many Polish and foreign companies. The office building, built by the European Leasing Fund, was erected in Podwale Street, next to the former city moat (designed by Dorota Jarodzka-Śródka, Kazimierz Śródka).

132. "Wratislavia Center" is an architectural complex providing space for hotels, offices and commercial facilities (it was designed by Leszek Łękawa, Jerzy Chmura, Marek Krupiński). The building was erected in the vicinity of St. Elisabeth's Church, on the plot surrounded by historical streets: Kiełbaśnicza, Św. Mikołaja and Rzeźnicza.

133. The building called "Millenium" in Strzegomska Street (designed by Wojciech Jarząbek and Artur Opala) is one of many office buildings being currently constructed in Wrocław. Annually about 6,000 new companies start up their business in the city (data from 2002).

134–135. Newly erected Wrocław hotels host foreign tourists visiting the city (about a million a year) as well as visitors coming to the capital city of the Lower Silesia on business. In the photographs are the "Mercure" hotel in Dominikański Square (designed by Edward Lach, Jan Matkowski, Anna Rumińska) and the "Park Plaza" hotel in Bolesława Drobnera Street (designed by Edward Lach with the team).

136. The International Airport and its passenger terminals (in Stanisława Skarżyńskiego Street, designed by Leszek Szostak, Krzysztof Wrzos) serve passengers of international and domestic routes.

Sources of quotations used in the text:

Joachim Bahlcke, *Śląsk i Ślązacy* (*Silesia and the Silesians*), translated by Michał Misiorny, Zofia Rybicka, Łukasz Żebrowski, Warsaw 2001.

Norman Davies, Roger Moorhouse, *Mikrokosmos. Portret miasta środkowoeuropejskiego* (*Microcosm. Portrait of a Central European City*), translated by Andrzej Pawelec, Cracow 2002.

Do nich przyszła Polska... Wspomnienia Polaków mieszkających we Wrocławiu od końca XIX wieku do 1939 roku (*Poland came to them...Memoirs of Poles living in Wrocław from the end of the 19th century to 1939*), compiled and elaborated by Alicja Zawisza, Wrocław 1993.

Karol Jonca, *Noc kryształowa i casus Herschela Grynszpana* (*The Crystal Night and the case of Herschel Grynszpan*), Wrocław 1998.

Ryszard Majewski, *Wrocław godzina „0"* (*Wrocław the „Zero" hour*), Wrocław 2000 (wspomnienia Luizy Hartmann) [Memoirs of Luiza Hartmann].

Paul Peikert, *Kronika dni oblężenia* (*Chronicle of the Siege*), compiled by Karol Jonca and Alfred Konieczny, Wrocław 1964.

Przesiedlenie ludności niemieckiej z Polski po II wojnie światowej w świetle dokumentów (*The Evacuation of the German population from Poland following the Second World War in the light of documents*), selection and compilation by Piotr Lippóczy, Tadeusz Walichnowski, Warsaw – Łódź 1982.

Walter Tausk, *Dżuma w mieście Breslau* (*Plague in the city of Wrocław*), translated by Ryszard Kincel, Warsaw 1973.

Trudne dni (*Hard days*), Wrocław 1960.

Wrocław liryczny (*Lyrical Wrocław*), selection and compilation by Marek Graszewicz, Marek Zybura, Wrocław 1997.

Wypędzeni ze Wschodu. Wspomnienia Polaków i Niemców (*Expelled from the East. Memoirs of Poles and Germans*), edited by Hans Jürgen Bömelburg, Renate Stössinger, Robert Traba, Olszyn 2001.

Sources of archival photographs:

Photographic Agency of Fighting Solidarity: p. 14
University Library of Wrocław: p. 9
Krystyna Gorazdowska: p. 11
Werner Güttel, *Breslau*, Berlin (1930?): pp. 5, 7.

Edition of the Polish text by Marcin Grabski, Olga Rutkowska
Translated by Andrzej Rossa, Agnieszka Ziajka-Małecka
Translation Consultant: Daniel Armitage
Cover and title page design by Tomasz Wachowiak

The album was created in cooperation with Wrocław City Promotion Office

© Copyright by VIA NOVA, Wrocław 2003

Wydawnictwo VIA NOVA
50-077 Wrocław, ul. Kazimierza Wielkiego 39, Poland
Phone: (0048 71) 344 23 77, Fax: (0048 71) 343 78 71
www.vianova.com.pl
ISBN 83-88649-68-X